ANIMALS OF THE RAIN FOREST

RAIN FORESTS

Lynn Stone

The Rourke Corporation, Inc.
Vero Beach, Florida 32964

Printed in the U.S.A.

PHOTO CREDITS
© Breck P. Kent: p. 12, 15; © James H. Carmichael: p. 18, 21; ©
Lynn M. Stone: cover, title page, p. 4, 7, 8, 10, 13, 17

Library of Congress Cataloging-in-Publication Data

Stone, Lynn M.
   Animals of the rain forest / by Lynn M. Stone
      p. cm. — (Discovering the rain forest)
   Includes index
   ISBN 0-86593-394-4
     1. Rain forest fauna—Juvenile literature. [1. Rain forest animals.]
  I. Title   II. series: Stone, Lynn M. Discovering the rain forest
QL112.S72 1994
591.909'52—dc20   94-20912
                               CIP

Printed in the USA   AC

TABLE OF CONTENTS

ANIMALS OF TROPICAL RAIN FORESTS

The warm, wet tropical rain forests of the world are **habitats**, or homes, for thousands of kinds of animals.

No one knows just how many kinds of animals live in the rain forests. Some of the most remote rain forests have never been studied!

The kind of animals in any area of tropical rain forest depend upon the forest's location. The largest tropical rain forests are in South America, West Africa and Southeast Asia.

The green, wet tropical rain forests
are homes to the world's
greatest animals

RAIN FOREST ANIMALS AROUND THE WORLD

Each tropical rain forest has its own variety of animals. Tigers, orangutans and clouded leopards, for example, live only in some of the Asian rain forests.

Forest elephants and gorillas live in African rain forests. South America has its specialties, too—dazzling **macaws**, smaller parrots and jaguars.

Even neighboring rain forests have somewhat different species of animals and plants.

Brightly colored macaws are the largest parrots

THE ANIMALS AND THE PLANTS

For survival, rain forest animals, large and small, depend upon forest plants. The plants provide shelter and food.

Animals either eat plants directly, or they eat other animals that have eaten plants.

Animals help plants by spreading plant seeds through their droppings. Bats and insects **pollinate** plants. Pollinating the flowers allows plants to make new plants.

This strange, spiny moth caterpillar lives on a diet of leaves

SURVIVING IN THE RAIN FOREST

Animals have special ways to survive in the tropical rain forests. Some iguana lizards have become **arboreal**. That means they live in trees.

Iguanas have plenty of company. Monkeys, sloths, parrots, toucans, and certain snakes and frogs are among the animals that live in the tree tops.

Many insects, lizards and frogs are masters of disguise. Their body color blends with their surroundings. They may look like sticks, leaves or bark.

A tree-climbing iguana loafs in the leaves of a rain forest canopy

The curious tamandua is an anteater

Orangutans prowl protected rain forests in Southeast Asia

INSECTS ·

The variety of insects in tropical rain forests is almost beyond belief. Some scientists think 80 million **species**, or kinds, of insects may live in rain forests.

Some of the most colorful insects are the thousands of species of tropical butterflies.

The "walkingsticks" make up another interesting group. These insects **mimic**, or look like, sticks!

The blue morpho is one of many colorful butterfly species in the rain forest

FROGS AND TOADS

Frogs and toads love the warmth, shade and **humidity**, or moisture, of tropical rain forests.

One of the most colorful frogs is the tiny poison-arrow frog. Its bright colors warn other animals away.

The poison-arrow frog is deadly to most **predators**, or hunters. South American Indians use the poison of poison-arrow frogs on the tips of their hunting arrows and darts.

16   *The poison-arrow frog, protected by its bright warning colors, is active by day*

SNAKES AND LIZARDS

Snakes and lizards live on the leafy floor of rain forests and in the trees above.

Snakes and lizards are predators. Like other rain forest hunters, they eat other animals.

Snakes catch birds, lizards, bats, rodents and other snakes. Lizards are insect-eaters.

Most snakes are **camouflaged** nicely. Their color blends into their surroundings.

The emerald tree boa is a perfect example. Its green skin matches the forest's green leaves.

The emerald tree boa is one of the rain forest's most colorful—and most camouflaged—animals

19

BIRDS

Most rain forest birds live in the **canopy**, or forest "roof." In this world of branches, vines and leaves, birds find seeds, fruits, insects and lizards. Many species nest in the canopy, too.

Birds are difficult to see from the forest floor. In clearings along the streams of South and Central American rain forests, however, watchers can see colorful parrots, toucans and hummingbirds.

Bright as a banana, the toucan's bill is a useful tool for tearing fruit from limbs

MAMMALS

Mammals live on the rain forest floor and in the crowns of the tallest trees. Monkeys swing from limb to limb while the anteater and armadillo prowl the ground below.

Great numbers of insects in the rain forests have resulted in great numbers of bats. Insects are the prey, or food, of most bat species.

Wild cats—jaguars, tigers, clouded leopards, ocelots—hunt prey in the rain forests, usually at night.

Glossary

arboreal (ar BOR ee uhl) — referring to plants and animals that live in trees

camouflage (KEM uh flahj) — to blend in with one's surroundings

canopy (KAN uh pee) — the "roof" of upper branches and leaves in a forest

habitat (HAB uh tat) — the special kind of area in which a plant or animal lives, such as the canopy of tropical rain forest

humidity (hu MID ih tee) — wetness or moisture in the air

macaw (muh KAW) — a group of large parrots found mostly in Central and South America

pollinate (PAH lin ate) — the process by which certain insects, bats and birds transfer pollen from one plant to another and help the plant to reproduce

predator (PRED uh tor) — an animal that kills other animals for food

species (SPEE sheez) — a certain kind of plant or animal within a closely related group; for example, a *scarlet* macaw

INDEX